SCIENCE PROJECTS

LIGHT

Trevor Day
Photography by Chris Fairclough

RSVP

**RAINTREE
STECK-VAUGHN**
P U B L I S H E R S
The Steck-Vaughn Company

Austin, Texas

Published by Raintree Steck-Vaughn Publishers, an imprint of Steck-Vaughn Company

Library of Congress Cataloging-in-Publication Data
Day, Trevor.
Light / Trevor Day.
    p.   cm.—(Science Projects)
    Includes bibliographical references and index.
    Summary: Introduces the concept of light and its properties through brief explanations followed by simple science experiments..
    ISBN 0-8172-4943-5
    1. Light—Experiments—Juvenile literature.
    2. Science projects—Juvenile literature.
    [1. Light—Experiments. 2. Experiments.]
    I. Title. II. Series.
    QC360.D39   1998
    535'.078—dc21   97-5991

Printed in Italy. Bound in the United States.
1 2 3 4 5 6 7 8 9 0 02 01 00 99 98

Picture acknowledgments
The publishers would like to thank the following for permission to reproduce their pictures **Bruce Coleman:** pages 4, 10 (Harald Lange), 20 (John Shaw); **NASA** page 4; **Oxford Scientific Films:** page 28 (Javed Jafferji); **Science Photo Library:** pages 14 (Bill Longcore), 32 (Harold Edgerton), 41 (Gordon Garradd), 42 top (Dr Jeremy Burgess), 42 bottom (Andrew McClenaghan), 44 (Françoise Sauze), cover (Mehau Kulyk); **Tony Stone Images:** pages 6 (David Muench), 8 (Glen Allison), 23 (Jeremy Horner), 38 (Tim Davis).

Illustrations: Julian Baker
Commissioned photography: Chris Fairclough

CONTENTS

SUNLIGHT

Light affects almost everything we do. Without light from the sun there would be no life on Earth. The planet would be cold and lifeless. The presence and absence of natural light—daytime and nighttime—governs when we choose to be awake and when we choose to sleep. If we want to continue working during nighttime, then we must rely on various sources of artificial light, like electric lights.

This photograph, taken from space, shows one half of the earth completely in daylight.

DAY AND NIGHT

MATERIALS
- a globe
- a flashlight

1. Place the globe on the table.

2. Ask a friend to stand about 6 ft. (2 m) away and hold the flashlight so that it shines directly on half of the globe. The flashlight represents the sun. Turn the globe so that your country is in the light of the flashlight and dim the rest of the room lights.

3. Notice how the side of the earth where your country is faces the "sun." This side is in sunlight, and here it is daytime.

The earth spins on its axis once every 24 hours. During part of that 24-hour period the place you live on the earth is turned toward the sun and is bathed in sunlight. It is daytime. During the other part of the 24-hour period the place you live is turned away from the sun and is in shadow. It is nighttime. The experiment below shows how the sun creates daytime and night-time.

This photograph shows half of the earth in daylight. The other half is in shadow, and therefore it is nighttime.

4. Looking from above, turn the globe counterclockwise slowly. This shows how the earth turns in space.

5. When you have made a half turn of the globe, you will notice that your country is now directed away from the "sun" and is in shadow. Now it is nighttime.

6. Keep turning the globe. Notice how the "sun" lights up the earth from east to west. Great Britain is in daylight before North America. The sun rises five hours earlier in London than it does in New York. This is why there are different time zones around the world.

SOURCES OF LIGHT

Very hot objects produce light. The sun —at 27 million° F (15 million° C)— provides most of the natural light on Earth, but there are other natural sources. Lightning, the sudden release of massive amounts of electrical energy, creates huge amounts of light. And burning objects—such as dry wood struck by lightning—produce a yellowy light. However, things do not have to be hot to generate light. Some animals produce their own light. Fireflies (also called glowworms) flash a green light from their backsides to attract a mate. They do this by using a natural chemical reaction—no heat is involved.

To help us see in poor light conditions, we have developed many artificial sources of light. In prehistoric times the first artificial sources were probably campfires. Since then, humans have harnessed fire as a source of light in candles, oil lamps, and gas lamps. Within the last hundred years or so, electricity has become our main source of artificial light. We take for granted the electric bulbs and fluorescent tubes we switch on every day.

The sun is the main source of natural light on Earth. You can see shafts of sunlight in this photograph.

MAKING A RAYBOX

1. Glue the block of wood to the base at one end of the shoe box.

2. Paint the inside of the shoe box, the lid, the piece of cardboard, and the wooden block with black paint.

3. Tape the flashlight to the wooden block so that its beam strikes the middle of the opposite end of the box. Cut five .75 in. x .08 in. (2 cm x 2 mm) vertical slits in this end of the box, the first in the center and the others spaced .08 in. (2 mm) apart on either side.

4. In the center of the piece of cardboard cut another slit .75 in. x .08 in. (2 cm x 2 mm).

5. Switch on the flashlight and darken the room. You will see five beams of light emerging from the raybox. Now clip the cardboard with one slit inside the end of the box so that the slit overlaps with the middle slit in the box. Now a single beam of light will emerge.

Why was it necessary to paint the inside of the raybox black?

MATERIALS

- a shoe box and lid
- a piece of cardboard the same size as the end of the shoe box
- 2 paper clips
- matte black poster paint
- a paintbrush
- a small, powerful, narrow-beam flashlight
- a block of wood about 4 in. (10 cm) long, 1.5 in. (4 cm) wide and .75 in. (2 cm) deep
- strong glue and dark tape
- a modeling knife
- a cutting board
- a metal straightedge

WARNING!

- Do not point the flashlight directly into anyone's eyes.
- Ask an adult to help with the knife and cutting board.

TRAVELING LIGHT

Light travels very fast indeed, much faster than sound. That is why you can see a flash of lightning before you hear the thunderclap that it creates. Sound covers just 1,100 ft. (340 m) in every second. Light, on the other hand, travels at 183,000 mi. (300,000,000 m) per second!

Under normal conditions, light travels in straight lines. You cannot usually see a beam of light from a flashlight, but you can see a small, bright spot when the beam hits something, like a wall.

This experiment shows how light travels.

You can see lightning before you hear the thunderclap because light travels faster than sound.

STRAIGHT TO THE POINT

MATERIALS
- a raybox and cardboard with one slit
- a hole punch
- three squares of dark cardboard
- modeling clay
- a straight knitting needle
- a sheet of white cardboard
- an incense stick
- safety matches

1. Set up the raybox.

2. Punch holes in the three squares at the same height as the beam from the raybox. Mount the squares in an upright position on a table, using small pieces of the modeling clay.

3. Position the squares so their holes are in a straight line. Check this by passing a straight knitting needle through the holes. Place the white square at the end of the row of black squares.

WARNING!
- Ask an adult to help with the incense and matches.

4. Darken the room. Shine the light beam through the holes. You should find a ray of light passing through the holes and forming a small bright spot on the white square.

5. Move the second square about .75 in. (2 cm) to one side. Now what can you see on the white square? Where does the ray of light fall? Does this tell you whether or not a light ray bends?

When a ray of light travels through the air, you cannot see it. You only see the presence of light when it strikes something—like the paper or the card. You can show rays of light traveling through the air by using small particles such as smoke particles. Light the incense stick, blow out the flame, and darken the room. Gently blow the smoke into the beam from the raybox. What do you see? Blow smoke into the ray of light passing through the squares. What do you see? What does this tell you about the way light travels?

DID YOU KNOW?

The distances in space are so enormous that we use light—the fastest thing we know—as a means of measuring them. The measurement is the light year—the distance that light travels in one year (nearly 6 trillion mi. [9.5 trillion km.]). The most distant objects we know are more than 13 billion light years away!

LETTING LIGHT IN

Everyday things respond to light in different ways. The passage of light through an object is called transmission. Some objects transmit light more readily than others.

Transparent materials allow all or nearly all light to pass through them. Such materials include clean air, clean water, and clear glass. We can see through them, and the image we see is very similar to the original object. Other materials are translucent. They allow some light through, but some of the light is scattered in all directions by particles within the material.

You can sometimes see through such materials, but they do not give a clear image. Frosted glass is an example of a translucent material.

Opaque materials do not allow light to pass through. They either absorb or reflect the light and so cast a strong shadow on the side opposite the light. Most everyday objects—including our bodies—are opaque.

This stained-glass window has some clear glass, which is transparent, but most of the glass is translucent. The leading between the pieces of glass is opaque.

SEEING THROUGH OBJECTS

Classifying objects as transparent, translucent, or opaque.

1. Lay the sheet of white paper on a table.

2. Using the books as props, set up the raybox so that it points downward at the paper. It should be about 12 in. (30 cm) from the paper. Switch on the raybox and darken the room.

3. Hold the material you are testing upright between the raybox and the paper.

4. Shine your raybox beam onto each of the materials in turn. Classify the materials as transparent, translucent, or opaque.

5. Record your results in a chart like the one at the bottom of the page. In column 2 insert "most," "some," "a little," or "none." In column 3 insert "transparent," "translucent," or "opaque" as appropriate.

6. List all the materials in order, with the most transparent at the top of the list, and the most opaque at the bottom.

Is your test of comparison among the different materials a fair test? If not, explain why. Are clouds in the sky transparent, translucent, or opaque? Explain your answer.

Material	How much light passes through	Nature of Material
Metal sheet		
paper tissue		
frosted glass		

11

ME AND MY SHADOW

A shadow forms when light from one direction strikes an opaque object. The light, unable to pass through the object, is stopped, and because light travels in straight lines, a shadow is cast on the far side of the object away from the light. The shadow forms an outline of the object.

Some shadows cast a sharp outline. Others have a less clear outline and have two parts—a dark inner region called the umbra and a lighter outer region called the penumbra. The penumbra receives some scattered light that makes the edge of the shadow blurred.

INVESTIGATING SHADOWS

1. Hold the sheet upright. Then place the slide projector about 6 ft. (2 m) away from the sheet and pointing at it.

2. Switch on the projector and darken the room.

3. Stand two of your friends of similar height and size between the light source and the sheet. One should be close to the sheet and to one side of the beam. The other should be farther away and to the other side.

MATERIALS

- a large white sheet
- a slide projector
- a table lamp with a shade

4. Move around to the far side of the sheet and look at the shadows cast by your two friends. Whose shadow is bigger? What happens to the sizes of the shadows when your friends change positions? Experiment to find out what determines the size of the shadow.

5. Now repeat what you did before, using the table lamp instead of the projector. Do these shadows have sharper or more blurred edges than before? What makes a shadow have sharp or blurred edges?

A SHADOW PLAY

1. Decide on a story you would like to perform using shadow puppets.

2. Cut the characters out of cardboard, making sure that each has a clear outline. Tape each shape onto a straw.

3. Hold up the sheet and then set up the slide projector about 7 to 10 ft. (2 to 3 m) from it. Darken the room. By holding the puppets between the projector and the sheet, you will be able to project a shadow onto the sheet.

4. Practice performing your play.

5. Try various effects such as changing the size of the shadow, making the shadows overlap, and making shadows appear and disappear.

6. Make sure that you do not cast your own shadows on the screen.

7. When you are happy with the result, ask your parents or friends to sit on the other side of the sheet while you perform your play.

13

HOW WE SEE THINGS

You may think that we see things around us by sending out a beam from our eyes to the object we are seeing. In fact, the reverse is true. We see by reflected light. Light from the sun, or some artificial source like a light bulb, bounces off the objects we are observing. This light enters our eyes and is detected by two sets of cells at the back of the eye in a layer called the retina. One of these sets of cells—called rods—are the ones we depend on when there is little light available. They do not produce color vision, but allow us to see in black-and-white and shades of gray. The other set of cells, called cones, detect color but they only operate when plenty of light is available. Rods and cones get their names from their shapes—cone cells are wider than rods.

This photograph shows the rods and cones of the eye greatly magnified. The orange-colored cells are the rods. The blue cells are the cones.

This simple experiment will show how we see by reflected light, and how the light-sensitive cells in our eyes respond to different amounts of light.

SEEING BY REFLECTED LIGHT

MATERIALS
- a shoe box and lid
- a sheet of cardboard
- matte black poster paint
- a paintbrush
- a modeling knife
- a cutting board
- any multicolored object

1. Paint the inside surface of the lid and box with black paint. Let it dry.

2. Carefully cut two slits about 1.5 in. x .75 in. (4 cm x 2 cm) in the lid of the shoe box, one slit at either end.

3. Place the multicolored object at one end of the box and replace the lid. Make sure that no light can enter the box except through the cut-out slits.

WARNING! Ask an adult to help with the modeling knife and cutting board.

6. Now remove the cardboard and ask your friend to identify the colors of the object by looking through the slit as before.

Can we see an object in complete darkness? Can we see color in poor light?

4. Place a sheet of cardboard over the slit at the same end as the multicolored object. Then get a friend to look into the slit at the other end of the box. Can your friend identify the object?

5. Now move the piece of cardboard slightly and allow a little light to enter. Can your friend identify the object now? Can he or she describe the colors of the object?

15

ON REFLECTION

We have already seen (pages 14–15) that most objects do not produce light of their own. Instead, we see these objects because of the light they reflect. It would be almost impossible for you to read this book in a darkened room. Switch on the light, however, and all is revealed. Light rays from the light bulb are reflected from the book and into your eyes.

The pages of a book reflect light well. Do this experiment to find out how well other things reflect light.

REFLECTIVE POWERS

MATERIALS
- a raybox and cardboard with 1 slit
- books
- a small flat, or plane, mirror
- two sheets of kitchen foil
- a sheet of black paper
- a sheet of white paper
- a large sheet of gray cardboard
- modeling clay
- a ruler

1. Using the books as props, set up the raybox so that it points downward at an angle. Switch on the raybox and darken the room.

2. Place a flat mirror face upward at the point where the beam from the raybox strikes the table.

3. You may be able to see the light beam striking the mirror and bouncing off at an angle. Whether or not the beam is visible, you can intercept it. Using modeling clay, mount the gray cardboard upright so that the reflected light beam strikes the cardboard.

4. Notice the size and brightness of the patch of light formed where the light beam strikes the cardboard. The smaller and brighter the patch of light, the better the reflective power of the material. Use a ruler to measure the size of the light patch. Make a note of the size and brightness of the patch and enter the observation in a chart like the one shown at the bottom of this page.

5. Take the two pieces of kitchen foil. Crumple one into a ball and then flatten it out again.

6. Now test the crumpled foil and the smooth foil and all the other materials in the same way as the mirror. In each case, make a note of the size and brightness of the patch of light produced by the reflected light.

7. Work out which surface is best at reflecting light and which is worst. Then place the other three surfaces in order in between.

What makes materials good at reflecting light? What makes them poor at reflecting light?

Material	Size and brightness of light spot
Mirror	
Smooth foil	
Wrinkled foil	
Black paper	
White paper	

MORE REFLECTIONS

You will have noticed in the experiment on pages 16–17 that when the light beam hits a mirror or reflective surface at an angle, it bounces off at another angle. The angle of the incoming beam is called the angle of incidence. The angle of the reflected beam is called the angle of reflection. You can measure the angles of incidence and reflection in this experiment.

MEASURING ANGLES

1. Use the ruler to draw a straight line near one edge of the sheet of cardboard. Measure the halfway point and mark it "O."

2. Now use the protractor and ruler to draw a second line at exactly 90° to the point that you marked "O" on the first line you drew. You should end up with a large "T" drawn on your card.

MATERIALS
- a raybox and cardboard with 1 slit
- a cork tile
- a sheet of white cardboard the same size as the cork tile
- 10 pins in assorted colors: 4 of one color and 3 pairs of different colors
- a small plane mirror
- modeling clay
- a ruler and a pencil
- a protractor
- colored pencils or felt-tip pens

3. Pin the corners of the paper or cardboard to the cork tile, using four pins of the same color.

4. Use modeling clay to mount the mirror upright exactly on the crossbar of the "T," facing the upright.

5. Switch on your raybox and darken the room. Position the raybox to the left of the mirror so that the light beam strikes the mirror at point "O."

6. Choose two pins of the same color and use them to carefully mark the path taken by the light beam before and after it bounces off the mirror.

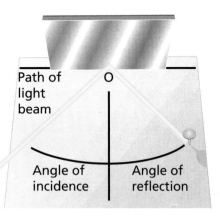

Path of light beam

O

Angle of incidence

Angle of reflection

7. Now change the angle at which the light beam strikes the mirror. Check that the light beam still strikes the mirror exactly at point "O." Use two pins of another color to mark the new positions of the light beam.

8. Repeat what you did before but with the light beam at a new angle.

9. Finally, what happens when you shine the light beam directly at the mirror along the upright of the "T?"

10. Turn on the light and remove the raybox and mirror. You are left with the "T" and three pairs of pins. With a ruler, draw straight lines in three different colors from each pin to point "O." Draw arrows on the lines to show the direction of the original light beams. Label the lines 1, 2, and 3.

11. Remove the pins and with a protractor measure the angle of incidence and the angle of reflection for each light beam. What do you notice about the two angles for each light beam?

MIRROR, MIRROR ...

A mirror is a superb reflector. Its surface is so smooth and shiny that it reflects light cleanly and gives a clear reflection. The mirrors in our homes are usually made of glass with a silvery coating on the back. Store or office windows often act like mirrors, too, especially those with tinted or reflective glass. But there are also natural mirrors. In still, sunny conditions the surface of a lake may act as a mirror.

A smooth lake gives an almost perfect reflection of this mountain scene.

YOUR MIRROR IMAGE

MATERIALS
● a large plane wall mirror

1. Look at your reflection in a large wall mirror. Where does your reflection appear to be—in front of or behind the mirror? Does the reflection appear to be the same distance away from the mirror as you are yourself or is it nearer or farther?

2. Wink your right eye. Which eye winked back at you in your reflection? Raise your left hand. Which hand was raised in your reflection?

3. Is your reflection the right way up and right way around, left to right? Is it the right way up but reversed left to right? Is it upside down and reversed left to right?

If you walk behind a mirror, you cannot find your reflection. It is not really where it appears to be. We call this reflection a virtual, or unreal, image.

MIRROR WRITING

MATERIALS
- a small plane mirror
- sheets of paper and a pencil

When you see images in a mirror, they look the wrong way around. When writing is reflected in a plane mirror, it, too, becomes reversed.

1. Write some capital letters on a sheet of paper. Hold it up to a mirror. Do any of the letters look the same when they are reversed?

2. Now try to write the letters so that they can be read correctly in a mirror. Check them in the mirror and keep correcting them until you get them right.

Ambulances and other emergency vehicles often have mirror-writing painted on the front. Why is this? Write "AMBULANCE" as it would appear on the front of the vehicle. How would "AMBULANCE" be written on the back? Why is this?

Symmetry

When an object can be divided along one or more lines into parts that are exact reflections of one another, the object is said to be symmetrical. Most animals have right and left halves that are mirror images of each other. This is called bilateral symmetry, and the animal is bilaterally symmetrical. We are bilaterally symmetrical, although our two halves are not exactly identical, as the photo of the boy's face below shows.

Normal face   *Two left halves*   *Two right halves*

MIRROR IMAGES

Not all mirrors are plane mirrors. Some mirrors bend outward. These are called convex mirrors. Some bend inward. These are called concave mirrors.

In this experiment we are going to use a raybox to find out what happens when rays of light are bounced off different types of mirror.

SEEING REFLECTED RAYS

1. Mount the plane mirror upright on the large white sheet of paper, using the modeling clay.

2. Place the raybox about 24 in. (60 cm) from the mirror and facing it. Switch it on and then darken the room. Examine the rays of light reflected from the mirror.

3. Now alter the position of the raybox to shine the five rays at the mirror from a different angle. This test should confirm the result you found in an earlier investigation (see pages 18–19). For a plane mirror, the angle of incidence and the angle of reflection are the same.

MATERIALS
- a raybox with five slits
- a large sheet of white paper
- a smaller sheet of white paper and a pencil
- a plane mirror, a concave mirror, and a convex mirror
- modeling clay

4. Replace the plane mirror with the concave mirror, and set up the raybox about 12 in. (30 cm) directly in front of the mirror.

5. What happens to the light rays when they are reflected from the concave mirror? Make a drawing of what you see.

Concave mirror

Look at this amusement park crazy mirror. The mirror makes the children look fatter and shorter. Is it concave or convex? If the mirror made them look long and thin, would it be concave or convex?

6. Replace the concave mirror with a convex mirror, and repeat the setup as for the concave mirror.

7. What happens to the reflected light rays now? Make a drawing of what you see.

Imagine you were looking in a concave mirror and your face was about 6 to 8 in. (15 to 20 cm) away from it. What would you see? Would your face appear larger or smaller than in real life? Check the answer for yourself by looking into your concave mirror.

If your face were about 6 to 8 in. (15 to 20 cm) away from the convex mirror what would you see?

Would your face appear larger or smaller than in real life? Check the answer for yourself by looking into your convex mirror.

There are many types of mirrors, and they do different jobs. What type of mirror—concave or convex— would be used as a shaving or makeup mirror? Why? What type of mirror would be used as a rearview mirror in a car? Why?

Convex mirror

UP PERISCOPE!

Light travels in straight lines, but we can make it go around corners by bouncing it off mirrors.

When light bounces off a flat mirror, it leaves the mirror surface at the same angle as it arrived. This property is used in the design of a periscope—a device used for seeing over or around an obstacle.

A periscope allows a person to observe an object from a hidden or protected position. There are many types of periscopes, but all include a tube with a mirror at either end. When used, the periscope tube is held upright and the top mirror is pointed toward the object to be observed. Light from the object reflects off the top mirror and then off the bottom mirror and into the eyes of the observer. Some periscopes have lenses that magnify the image and make the object appear larger.

Periscopes are especially useful for military purposes. They enable someone in a submarine, an armored tank, or a dugout trench to see what is going on above without being seen.

MAKING A PERISCOPE

MATERIALS
- an empty long, narrow, cardboard kitchen foil box
- heavy-duty dark tape
- a sheet of cardboard
- a ruler
- a pencil
- a protractor
- a modeling knife and cutting board
- two plastic mirrors about 3.5 in. x 2.5 in. (9 cm x 6 cm)

1. Carefully remove the serrated cutting edge of the box. Then use a strip of tape to seal the exposed slit in the box.

2. Draw a right-angled triangle with two sides of length 2 in. (5 cm) on the sheet of cardboard, using the protractor.

3. Cut out the triangle shape and use it to draw straight diagonal lines on the opposite sides at either end of the box, as shown here. It is important that the diagonal lines are exactly opposite each other.

4. Carefully cut a slot wide enough for the mirrors along each diagonal line. These are the 45° slots into which the mirrors will be mounted.

5. Cut two rectangular holes about 2.5 in. x 1.5 in. (6 cm x 4 cm) at the ends of two sides as shown.

Viewing port

Mirror

6. Now slide a mirror into each diagonal slot so that the mirror surface can be seen through each viewing port.

7. Secure the mirrors by taping them into place. Use tape to seal any gaps. This prevents stray light from entering. Your periscope is now complete.

8. Test your periscope by viewing an object from below table level. Is the image you see through the periscope upside down, back to front, or the correct way around?

WARNING!

- Ask an adult to help you remove the sharp cutting edge of the box and to help you with the knife.

- Do not point your periscope at the sun.

KALEIDOSCOPES

Look into a mirror and you will see one image of yourself. Look in a mirror and hold up another smaller mirror facing the other one, and you will see a never-ending series of mirrors.

By making mirrors face each other you can make multiple images and create marvelous patterns from their reflections. A kaleidoscope is a device that uses several mirrors facing inward to bounce light off each other. When an object inside the kaleidoscope moves, it produces many reflections in a symmetrical and beautiful pattern.

Two plane mirrors facing each other create an infinite number of images of the apple by reflecting alternate sides of the apple.

MATERIALS

- a piece of cardboard about 10 in. x 6 in. (25 cm x 15 cm)
- a glue stick
- a ruler
- a pencil
- a metal straightedge
- a modeling knife & cutting board
- a sheet of reflective silver plastic wrapping
- a paper tissue or soft cloth
- dark tape
- a transparent or translucent sandwich box lid
- two short strips of wood at least .5 in. (1.5 cm) thick
- tiny pieces of colored paper or other small colorful objects

MAKING A KALEIDOSCOPE

1. With a pencil, mark off the cardboard along its 6 in. (15 cm) length into three panels each 2 in. (5 cm) wide.

2. Score along the lines with the modeling knife, being careful not to cut through the cardboard.

3. On the unscored side glue the sheet of silver wrapping, shiny side up. Smooth the foil flat with a piece of tissue or soft cloth.

4. Now fold the cardboard into a triangular tube shape with the mirror surface on the inside.

5. Join the edges of the cardboard together with dark tape. Make sure there is a complete seal along the join so that no light enters.

6. Set the sandwich box lid on the two strips of wood next to a window. Then sprinkle on the tiny pieces of colored paper.

7. Place the tube on top of the pieces of paper on the sandwich box lid. Look through the tube and see the patterns produced by the reflections inside the tube. How many sides do the patterns have?

8. Tap the sandwich box lid or turn the tube to change the pattern and color combinations.

9. Experiment with other small objects, like crystals or small beads.

WARNING!
● Ask an adult to help you use the knife.

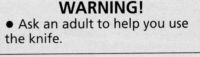

DID YOU KNOW?

The image you see inside a kaleidoscope is an example of radial symmetry. With this type of symmetry, matching parts are arranged around a central point, or axis. Some animals and plants show radial symmetry— for example, a sea urchin, and the petals of a daisy or rose.

BENDING LIGHT

Have you ever jumped into a swimming pool and then found that the water was deeper than you thought it looked? This effect is caused by the bending of light rays when they travel from one transparent substance to another. This bending is called refraction.

How does this bending of light come about? Light travels fast in air, but more slowly in water, glass, and other transparent liquids and solids. However, its speed is still very high: in water, for example, it travels at approximately 738,000,000 ft. (225,000,000 m) a second.

Water slows light rays in much the same way that it slows down your legs when you walk through a swimming pool. Water is much denser than air. Transparent plastic is denser still.

So light travels fastest in air, more slowly in water, and even more slowly through plastic. This slowing of light does not have a noticeable effect when it passes at right angles through the boundary between one substance to another. But when light is hitting the boundary at an angle, then the light is bent.

> **DID YOU KNOW?**
>
> **A mirage is a false view of the sky that looks like a pool of water on the ground. It is caused by a layer of hot air close to the ground, refracting light rays from the sky. You can sometimes see mirages above roads on hot days.**

This fisherman must aim his spear at a different point from where the fish appears to be to allow for refraction.

BENDING LIGHT THROUGH WATER AND PLASTIC

1. Place a few drops of milk in the water in the aquarium to make it turn slightly murky.

2. Using the box and books as props, arrange the raybox so that it is pointing downward at an angle to the water. Darken the room and switch on the raybox. What happens to the beam of light where it strikes the water's surface? If you cannot see the light before it enters the water, hold a glowing incense stick below the beam.

3. Now move the light source so that the beam of light enters at an angle through the side of the container. What happens to the light beam where it strikes the plastic and then enters the water?

4. In the first part of this investigation you made a light beam travel from air straight into water. In the second part, you made the light beam travel from air, through plastic, and then into water. Was light bent in the same direction and by the same amount in each case? If not, can you explain why?

BENDING MORE LIGHT

Light is bent, or refracted, when it passes from one transparent medium to another. The amount of refraction is related to the density of the substance. Those that are denser slow the light more and cause more refraction. Substances that are less dense slow light less and cause less refraction.

BENDING LIGHT THROUGH LIQUIDS

1. Fill three of the containers to two-thirds full with the following: one with water to which a few drops of milk have been added; the second with a strong salt solution to which a few drops of food coloring have been added; the third with corn oil. Leave the fourth empty.

2. Using the books and protractor, fix the raybox so that it points downward at a 45° angle.

WARNING!
- Ask an adult to help with the incense stick and matches.

MATERIALS
- a raybox and cardboard with 1 slit
- boxes and books as props
- a protractor
- four transparent square or rectangular straight-sided containers
- two teaspoons
- an incense stick and a box of safety matches
- corn oil
- food coloring
- milk
- water
- salt
- a notebook and a pencil

3. Darken the room and shine the light beam into the container of milky water. Ensure that the beam shines directly into the liquid and not through the side of the container. If you have difficulty seeing the beam of light before it enters the water, hold a glowing incense stick below the beam.

4. Measure the angle by which the light is bent at the boundary between air and water. Record your result.

5. Repeat the test with the salted water and then with the oil, recording your results as you go.

6. Which liquid bent the light the most? Which bent the light the least? What does this tell you about the densities of the three liquids? Which is the most dense and which is the least dense?

7. For a spectacular finish, carefully pour all three liquids into the fourth container like this: Fill the fourth container one-third full with the most dense liquid. Now very gently pour the next most dense liquid onto the back of a spoon held just above the first liquid. You should be left with two separate layers, one floating on the other.

8. Repeat this, using the other spoon and the least dense liquid, so that this forms a third layer floating on top of the other two.

9. Shine your angled beam of light down into the container and you will see a spectacular sight!

TAKING A SNAPSHOT

A series of high-speed photographs of pole vaulter David Tork in action

If you have ever looked inside a camera, you will have seen that it is a lightproof box with a small hole covered by a lens on one side and photographic film on the other. The film records an image as seen through the lens.

The first cameras were based on a device called the camera obscura (Latin for "dark chamber"). This was a lightproof room with a small hole in one wall. Light from outside shone through the hole, forming an upside-down image of the view outside. This was projected onto the inner wall opposite the hole.

The Italian inventor Leonardo da Vinci (1452–1519) was one of the first to describe how the camera obscura worked.

A SIMPLE CAMERA OBSCURA

The term *camera obscura* refers to an enclosed dark room or box into which light passes through a small hole or lens to produce an image on ground glass or paper. The problem with the portable camera obscura, invented in Italy in the 16th century, was that the image could not be recorded.

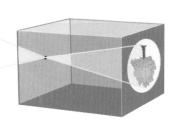

MAKING A PINHOLE CAMERA

1. Use the hammer and nail to punch a hole in the center of the base of the can. Cover this hole with two strips of tape.

2. Use a pin to pierce a small hole in the tape through the center of the hole in the can.

3. Wrap the circle of wax paper tightly over the open end of the can and secure it in place with the rubber band. Make sure that the paper makes a flat surface. The paper is the viewing screen.

4. Stand 13 to 16 ft. (4 to 5 m) away from a bright window. Drape the dark cloth over your head and over the camera's viewing screen.

5. Hold the camera at arm's length and point the pinhole at the window. Look at the viewing screen. What do you see? Is the picture upside-down or the right way up? Is the picture dim or bright? Is it larger or smaller than the window? Is the picture clear or blurred?

6. Now take the pin and pierce four new holes around the original pinhole. What do you see on the viewing screen now?

7. Use the nail to enlarge the original pinhole so that it is the same size as the nail hole in the can. Now what do you see on the viewing screen?

MATERIALS

- a medium-sized empty can
- a dark cloth, 3 ft. x 3 ft. (1 m x 1 m)
- a pin
- a hammer and a large nail
- scissors
- heavy-duty dark tape
- a circle of wax paper slightly larger than the base of the can
- a rubber band

WARNING!

- Ask an adult to help you use the hammer and nails.
- Do not point your pinhole camera at the sun.

LENSES

We have seen (pages 28–31) how a ray of light passing through flat transparent plastic or glass is bent, or refracted. A lens is a piece of transparent glass or plastic with a curved surface. Convex lenses bend outward and concave lenses bend inward.

In the experiment below you will find out what happens to light when it passes through convex and concave lenses.

LIGHT THROUGH A LENS

1. First attach the convex lens upright to the white cardboard using the modeling clay.

2. Then set the raybox so that it faces the lens, about 6 in. (15 cm) away from it.

3. Turn on the raybox and darken the room. What happens to the rays of light when they pass through the convex lens? Draw the path of the light before and after it passes through the lens.

4. Now repeat the experiment with the concave lens. What happens to the rays of light this time? Draw the path of the light before and after it passes through the lens.

MATERIALS

- a raybox with five slits
- a rectangular convex lens and a rectangular concave lens
- a piece of white cardboard
- paper and a pencil
- modeling clay

There is a lens near the front of your eye. When you look at an object, light rays from the object are refracted by the transparent front of the eye—the cornea—and by the lens of the eye. The light rays are focused to form an image on the retina at the back of the eye. The image on the retina is upside down and back to front. This information is sent along the optic nerve to the brain. The brain then "turns" the image the right way up.

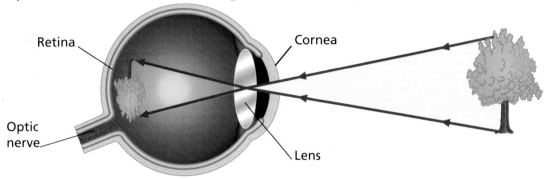

Retina

Cornea

Optic nerve

Lens

HOW WE SEE

1. Point the magnifying glass at a brightly lit window and hold a sheet of paper upright a short distance behind the magnifying glass lens.

2. Move the paper toward and away from the magnifying glass until a clear image of the window appears on the paper.

3. Is the image of the window larger or smaller than the window itself? Is the image upside down or the right way up? The magnifying glass represents the lens of the eye. What part of the eye does the paper represent?

MATERIALS

- a magnifying glass
- a sheet of plain paper

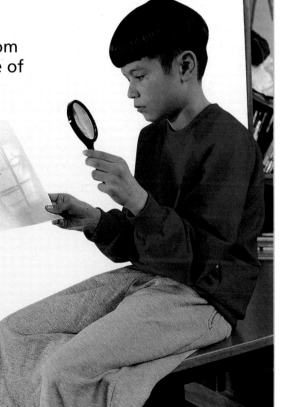

WARNING!

- Do not look at the sun directly or point your magnifying glass at the sun.

IN FOCUS

The lens in the eye is able to change shape so that near or far objects can be precisely focused on the retina. When you look at a near object, the lens bulges and bends the light rays more in order to focus the near object on the retina. When you look at a more distant object, the lens narrows, the light rays are bent less, and the distant object is focused on the retina.

Some people have eyes that do not focus properly, so they wear glasses or contact lenses. People who are nearsighted can see well close up but are unable to focus on objects a long way off. Such people have eyeballs that are too long or lenses of the eye that are too thick. This causes the light to be refracted too much when it enters the eye. When these people look at a distant object the image is focused in front of the retina so that the image on the retina is blurred.

Nearsighted

For distant viewing, point of clear focus is in front of retina

Farsighted

For close viewing, point of clear focus is behind retina

People who are farsighted can see distant objects well but are unable to focus on near objects. They either have eyeballs that are too short or lenses of the eye that are too thin. When looking at a near object, the light entering the eye is not refracted enough. The image is focused behind the retina and as a result is blurred.

This investigation will show which types of lens are needed to correct farsighted and nearsighted vision.

CORRECTING EYE PROBLEMS

1. Make two supports for the cardboard out of modeling clay. These should hold it upright but allow you to move it back and forth.

2. Hold the magnifying glass between the lamp and the cardboard about 3 ft. (1 m) away from the lamp. Switch on the lamp.

3. Move the cardboard toward and away from the magnifying glass until a clear image of the lamp appears on the cardboard.

4. Now move the paper backward away from the lamp so that the image of the lamp is slightly out of focus. This represents the situation for a nearsighted person—the image is being focused in front of the cardboard (or the retina).

5. Experiment by first placing the convex lens and then the concave lens just in front of the magnifying lens. Which lens sharpens the image on the cardboard?

6. With the magnifying glass in position move the paper forward so that the image of the lamp is once more in focus. Now move the paper forward toward the lamp a bit more so that the image is slightly out of focus. This represents the situation for a farsighted person—the image is being focused behind the cardboard (or the retina).

7. Experiment again by first placing the convex lens and then the concave lens just in front of the magnifying lens. Which lens sharpens the image on the cardboard?

8. Which type of lens—convex or concave—is used in eyeglasses to correct nearsighted vision? Which type of lens is used to correct farsighted vision?

SEEING DOUBLE

Our eyes are set on the front of the head, facing forward. Having two eyes in the fronts of our heads helps us judge distances. Many animals that hunt for their food have eyes in the fronts of their heads, too. This enables them to judge how far away their prey is when they are stalking and chasing. On the other hand, the animals that they are hunting often have their eyes set on each side of their heads. This enables them to see all around them and to spot any would-be predators.

Each of our eyes sees a slightly different view of the same object. This gives our vision "depth"— we see things in three dimensions (3-D). It is easy to show this by simple investigation.

An owl needs both eyes at the front of its head so that it can judge distances accurately when hunting.

TWO VIEWS OF THE WORLD

1. Extend your right arm and hold up your thumb. Close your left eye and look at your thumb with your right eye.

2. Line up your thumb with a distant object—a tree or a church spire, for example.

3. Without moving your thumb, close your right eye, open your left, and look at your thumb. Which way has your thumb appeared to move?

4. Keeping your thumb still, close your left eye, open your right, and look at your thumb. Which way has your thumb moved now?

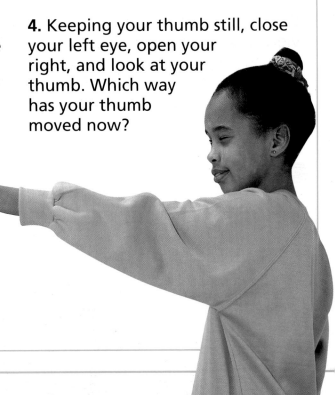

FIELD OF VISION

The area we see with each eye is called the field of vision. The fields of vision of our two eyes overlap. See this for yourself.

1. Hold your head still and close your left eye. Look straight ahead with your right eye.

2. Now extend your right arm out to your side at a height level with your shoulder. Hold up your thumb.

3. Keeping your arm straight, gradually move your arm forward. Notice the point at which your thumb comes into view.

4. Keep your head still, with your left eye closed and your right eye looking straight ahead.

5. Extend your left arm out to your side and level with your shoulder. Hold up your thumb and slowly swing your left arm forward. Notice the point at which your left thumb comes into view. For your right eye, is the field of view wider on your left or on your right?

6. Repeat the above but with your left eye open and your right eye closed. For your left eye, is the field of view wider on your left or on your right?

OVERLAPPING VIEWS

If you could plot the field of view of your two eyes, it would look something like the picture below. There is an area in the center of your field of vision that both eyes can see. This is your overlapping field of vision. What keeps the fields of vision of your two eyes from overlapping more?

Area seen by left eye

Area seen by both eyes

Area seen by right eye

MAKING RAINBOWS

We call the light we receive from the sun white light. However, it is not simply white. It is composed of six main colors: red, orange, yellow, green, blue, and violet. This sequence is called the color spectrum. We see these colors when sunlight shines through raindrops and creates rainbows. The raindrops refract white light and cause the separation of colors. Each color is refracted by a slightly different amount as it passes into and then out of a raindrop. Red light is bent the least and violet light the most.

We can create a spectrum by refracting sunlight through water.

MATERIALS

- a glass of water
- a large sheet of white paper
- a cardboard box

MAKING A RAINBOW

1. Choose a clear morning at a time when the sun is fairly low in the sky.

2. Place a glass of water on a box about 13 ft. (4 m) away from a window that is receiving direct sunlight. You should be able to see the rainbow spread of colors on the floor as the sunlight is refracted through the glass of water.

3. Place the sheet of white paper where the rainbow falls and try to identify the colors in the rainbow.

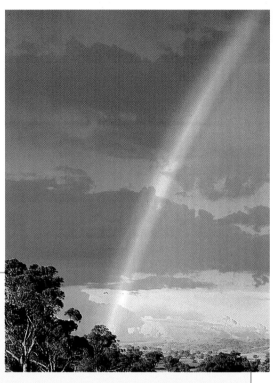

Rainbows are produced when sunlight is refracted through tiny drops of rain.

TURNING COLORS WHITE

You can change the rainbow colors back into white.

MATERIALS

- a piece of cardboard about 8 in. x 8 in. (20 cm x 20 cm)
- a compass
- scissors
- a protractor & a ruler
- two sharp pencils, one short, one long
- colored pencils

1. On the cardboard use the compass to draw a circle 6 in. (15 cm) across. Cut out the circle with scissors.

2. Use the protractor and a pencil and ruler to divide the circle into six equal sections (each is a slice at an angle of 60°). Color the sections in the order: red, orange, yellow, green, blue, and violet.

3. Push a short pencil, point first, through the hole in the center of the circle.

4. Spin the circle like the top and watch the colors appear to merge to white or off-white. When the circle slows, the colors reappear.

5. When the top is spinning fast, our eyes cannot separate the different colors. They merge and are "seen" by the brain as white.

SUBTRACTING COLORS

When light reaches an object, some light is reflected and some is absorbed. However, the object will usually reflect and absorb light of different colors in differing amounts. This is what gives the object its color. In daylight, most objects we see around us are colored by the light they reflect, not the light they produce.

When sunlight falls on a sandy beach, for example, the sand absorbs all the different colors in the light except yellow. It reflects the yellow light into our eyes, so the sand appears yellow. White objects look white in sunlight because they reflect all colors equally and absorb very little. Black objects appear black because they absorb almost all the light they receive and they reflect very little.

Although white light is really made up of the six colors of the color spectrum, it is easier to think of white light as made up of three main colors—red, green, and blue. These are the primary colors of light. All other colors (except black) can be made by mixing these colors in different amounts.

The color of this caterpillar's skin warns predators that it is poisonous.

Filters are made from transparent colored material. A red filter allows only red light to shine through, a blue only blue light, and so on. Each filter blocks all other parts of the color spectrum. Filters are used to create special effects in stage shows such as rock concerts. You may have noticed how colored spotlights make performers' clothes appear to change color in strange ways. There are simple rules that govern these color changes.

The color of this male oak beauty moth helps it blend with its surroundings.

USING FILTERS

1. Do the investigation in natural light or under ordinary room lighting. Tape the red filter or cellophane over the lens of the flashlight.

2. Switch on the flashlight and shine the resulting red beam at objects of various colors from a distance of about 3 ft. (1 m). In each case make a note of the color the object appears to be when viewed by red light. Enter your results in a chart like the one below.

Colour of Object \ Colour of Filter	Red	Green	Blue
White			
Red			
Green			
Blue			
Yellow			
Orange			

3. Repeat the investigation, using a green filter in place of the red and again using the blue filter.

4. What happens when you shine a colored beam onto a white surface? What happens when you shine it on to a different primary color? What do you see if you shine it onto a nonprimary color such as yellow or orange?

ADDING COLORS

Filters block out some of the light that passes through them. Blue filters block out all the other colors of light except blue. If a blue filter is placed over a spotlight, it creates a beam of light the same color as the filter. But what happens when different colored beams of light are mixed together?

As we saw on pages 42–43, the three primary colors of light are red, green, and blue. Color television works by mixing together these three colors to create all the other colors. The picture on the screen is made up of tiny dots or stripes of red, green, and blue. The combination of illuminated dots or stripes gives the color of that part of the screen. When you view the screen from a distance, the colored dots or stripes merge to create a natural-looking picture.

MIXING COLORS

MATERIALS
- three flashlights
- red, green, and blue filters or cellophane
- tape
- a white wall or large sheet of white cardboard

1. Cover the lenses of three flashlights with the different-colored filters or cellophane.

2. Check that the three beams of light—one red, one green, one blue—are of roughly equal brightness. If not, add more layers of cellophane until all three are of equal brightness.

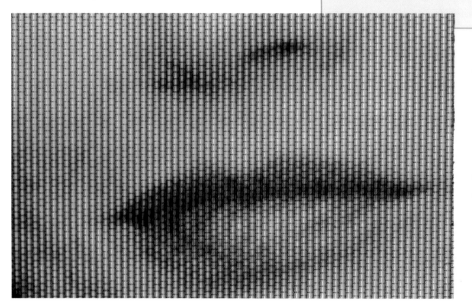

A closeup of a television screen reveals the red, green, and blue dots that together make up all the colors you see. Any single point on the screen is made up of varying proportions of these three colors.

4. What is the color of the region where the red and green beams overlap? Describe the color of the region where the blue and red beams overlap. The proper name for this color is magenta. Describe the color of the region where blue and green beams overlap. The proper name for this color is cyan.

5. What color would you expect the central area—where all three beams overlap—to be? Is it this color? If not, can you explain why?

3. Now darken the room. Shine all three flashlights at the white wall or cardboard so that all three beams overlap in a neat arrangement.

Mixing colored lights is not the same as mixing colored inks or paints. With printing inks and paints, the primary colors are cyan, magenta, and yellow. Compare these colors with those you discovered by overlapping red, green, and blue flashlight beams. What do you notice? The many colors printed on the white paper of this book are made by mixing together the three primary colors of printing inks. On the printed page, combining different amounts of the three primary colors (plus black) produces all the other colors you see.

Yellow

Magenta

Cyan

45

GLOSSARY

Color The way our eyes perceive the different components of white light. The range of colors forms the light spectrum: red, orange, yellow, green, blue, and violet.

Concave Curving inward, as in the bowl of a spoon. The shape of certain lenses and mirrors.

Convex Curving outward, as in the back of a spoon. The shape of certain lenses and mirrors.

Cornea The transparent outer layer at the front of the eye. It bends (refracts) light slightly.

Focus The point at which light rays meet after they have been reflected or refracted. An image looks sharp when it is in focus.

Image When light rays are bounced (reflected) off a mirror or bent (refracted) through a lens, they form a copy of an object. This copy is called an image.

Kaleidoscope A device that uses several mirrors, all facing inward. The many reflections inside form attractive symmetrical patterns.

Lens A curved piece of glass or other transparent material that forms an image by bending (refracting) light rays.

Light A special form of energy that can be seen by our eyes. (It is also called visible electromagnetic radiation.)

Opaque Used to describe a substance that does not allow light to pass through.

Periscope A device that reflects light through two right angles and so enables a person to see over or around obstacles.

Pigment A substance that gives color to the cells and tissues of plants and animals.

Primary color A pure color that cannot be made by mixing other colors. All nonprimary colors can be made by mixing together the three primary colors in different proportions.

Prism A triangular piece of glass or other transparent material used to split white light into the color spectrum.

Ray The straight path followed by light as it travels from its source.

Reflection Light rays bouncing off a surface. It is also the name of the image of an object seen in a mirror.

Refraction Light rays being bent as they pass from one transparent material to another.

Retina The light-sensitive layer at the back of the eye. The image is formed on this after light has passed through the lens.

Shadow A dark region that forms beyond an opaque object where it blocks out light.

Spectrum The range of colors that make up white light. The spectrum can be produced by bending (refracting) white light through a prism.

Symmetrical The term for an object that can be divided along one or more lines into parts that are exact mirror reflections of one another.

Translucent Used to describe a substance that allows some light to pass through. Objects cannot be seen clearly through such substances.

Transparent Used to describe a substance that allows all or nearly all light to pass through. Objects can be seen clearly through such substances.

FURTHER INFORMATION

BOOKS

Catherall, Ed. *Exploring Light.* Exploring Science. Austin, TX: Raintree Steck-Vaughn, 1990.

Kerrod, Robin. *Light & Sound.* Let's Investigate Science. Tarrytown, NY: Marshall Cavendish, 1995.

Rowe, Julian. *Colorful Light.* Danbury, CT: Children's Press, 1993.

CD – ROMS

Exploring Science – Light and Sound
Raintree Steck-Vaughn, 1997.

ANSWERS TO QUESTIONS

Answers to questions asked in the projects.

Pages 6–7 The inside of the raybox was painted black to prevent light rays being reflected off the box walls, so producing scattered beams of light rather than the narrow beams required.

Pages 8–9 When you move the second square the spot of light disappears from the white square and falls on the second square. This tells you that a ray of light does not bend. It travels in a straight line. When you blow smoke into a beam of light you can see it traveling in a straight line.

Pages 10–11 This is not a fair test because the sheets of materials may not all be of the same thickness. Also they may not be held exactly the same distance from the raybox each time. Clouds in the sky are translucent. They allow some light through, but you cannot see through them.

Pages 12–13 The shadow of the friend nearest the projector is bigger. When your friends change position, their shadows change in size. The smaller becomes larger, and vice versa. When using the table lamp in place of the projector, the shadow edges are more blurred. The brighter the lighting, the sharper the edges of the shadows, and vice versa.

Pages 14–15 With the unaided eye, we cannot see objects in complete darkness. We cannot see color in poor light; we can see only black, white, and shades of gray.

Pages 16–17 Materials that are good at reflecting light are smooth, flat, and shiny or light-colored. Materials that are poor at reflecting light are rough, crinkled, and dull or dark-colored.

Pages 18–19 When you shine the beam directly at the mirror along the upright of the "T," the light beam is directed back along its line of travel. The angle that the light beam strikes and bounces off the mirror is the same.

Pages 20–21 The capital letters A, H, I, M, O, T, U, V, W, X, and Y remain the same when reversed. Emergency vehicles sometimes have mirror writing on the front so that drivers in cars ahead see the writing reflected the right way around in their mirrors. On the back of the vehicles the writing is the correct way around.

Pages 22–23 When the light rays are reflected from a concave mirror they converge. When they are reflected from a convex mirror they diverge. Your face would appear larger in a concave mirror and smaller in a convex mirror. A concave mirror would be used as a shaving mirror because it makes a person's face appear larger. A convex mirror would be used as a rearview mirror because it gives a wide field of view.

Pages 24–25 The image in a periscope is the correct way around.

Pages 26–27 The pattern has six sides.

Pages 28–29 When the beam strikes the water it is bent downward. When it strikes the plastic and then the water, it will be bent upward. The light beam is bent more when it enters plastic and then water because plastic is denser than water and bends the light more.

Pages 30–31 Salted water bends light the most and so is the most dense; oil bends the light least and so is the least dense.

Pages 32–33 The picture is upside down and reversed left to right. It is smaller than the window itself and is dim but clear. The five pinholes in the pinhole camera produce five images of the window. The large hole produces a bright picture of the window, but it is blurred.

Pages 34–35 When light rays pass through a convex lens they converge. When they pass though a concave lens they diverge. The image of the window is smaller than the window itself and is upside down. The paper represents the retina of the eye.

Pages 36–37 For a nearsighted person, a concave lens will improve vision. For a farsighted person, a convex lens will improve vision.

Pages 38–39 The thumb appears to move first to the right and then to the left. The field of view of the right eye is wider on the right hand side. Your nose stops the field of vision overlapping more.

Pages 42–43 When you shine a colored beam onto a white surface it appears to be the same color as the light beam. When you shine the beam on to a primary color, a nonprimary color is produced; when you shine it on to a nonprimary color the surface takes on the color of the light beam.

Pages 44–45 The region where the red and green beams overlap is yellow. The central area where all three beams overlap is white. If it is not white it is because one of the colored beams is brighter than the others. The overall lighting within the room will also affect the central color.

INDEX